NASHVILLE

IN PHOTOGRAPHS

NASHVILLE

IN PHOTOGRAPHS

AUBREY C. WATSON

GRAMERCY BOOKS
NEW YORK

© 2006 Salamander Books
An imprint of Anova Books Company Ltd
151 Freston Road, London, W10 6TH

Published by Gramercy Books,
an imprint of Random House Value Publishing,
a division of Random House, Inc., New York,
by arrangement with Anova Books, London.

Gramercy is a registered trademark and the
colophon is a trademark of Random House, Inc.

Random House
New York • Toronto • London • Sydney • Auckland
www.randomhouse.com

Printed and bound in China

A catalog record for this title is available from the Library
of Congress.

ISBN-13: 978-0-517-22876-0
ISBN-10: 0-517-22876-9

10 9 8 7 6 5 4 3 2 1

Credits
Editor: Martin Howard
Designer: Cara Rogers
Production: Kate Rogers
Reproduction: Anorax Imaging Ltd

Additional captions
Page 1: Andrew Jackson Statue at Night (page 21)
Page 2: Crocker Springs Bed and Breakfast (page 55)

Acknowledgments
The author would like to thank Karina McDaniel, Barbara Parker,
Maggie Jackson, Belinda Leslie, Paula Hankins, David Underwood,
Pete Fisher, Gina Keltner, Brandon Taylor, Bill Reynolds, Jack and Bev
Spangler, Cheekwood, Baptist Sports Park, The Hermitage, Travellers
Rest, The Nashville Zoo, The Wild Horse Saloon, Opryland Hotel,
and The Grand Ole Opry.

Picture Acknowledgments
All photographs © Anova Image Library/Aubrey C. Watson, except
for pages 20, 21 (top), and 110, which are © Anova Image
Library/Karina McDaniel

Contents

INTRODUCTION

Nashville may be a city of only 600,000 souls—not even the biggest in Tennessee—but it is a small town with a big voice. Like New Orleans, it is a city that has become synonymous with a music style it has made its own. Nashville is the home of country and is known worldwide as Music City, USA. If popular music is America's gift to the modern world, then Nashville is one of its most important sources. And while the music industry and the tourism it attracts are the most important part of the city's income, Nashville also boasts printing, publishing, automobile, healthcare, financial, and manufacturing industries.

The city is situated in a region referred to as "Middle Tennessee." The geology of the state is such that there are three grand divisions from the Unaka

Mountains in the east to the alluvial delta country in the west along the Mississippi River. Middle Tennessee lies in the central basin surrounded by the Highland Rim. The mild climate, abundant rainfall, and fertile hills and valleys have attracted people to the region since the first natives built a village on the bluffs of the Cumberland River as early as 8,000 BC. When these settlements disappeared around AD 1450, Middle Tennessee became a neutral hunting area. Woodland bison, elk, deer, turkey, and beaver were a plentiful source of meat and hides for the Cherokee, Chocktow, Chickasaw, Creek, and Shawnee Indian tribes.

▼ **Nashville Skyline at Night:** *What began as a tiny trading post is now one of the United States' most individual and dynamic cities. Attracting musical talent, business, and tourists from across the globe, Nashville is a modern city with a great twenty-first century skyline and the atmosphere of a friendly small town.*

The first Europeans to reach the area were French fur traders from New Orleans. In about 1710 one of them—Jean duCharleville—established a trading post in an abandoned Shawnee camp at a salt lick north of present-day Downtown. It became known as "French Lick" and continued as a small trading post for the next half-century or so. A French-Canadian by the name of Timothe DeMontbrun (his name was anglicized to Timothy Demonbreun) arrived at French Lick around 1769 and set about building a successful fur and mercantile business. He represented the beginning of a permanent settlement.

▶ **General Jackson:** *The showboat, which carries the name of its famous predecessor, is seen here docked on the east side of the Cumberland River to take on passengers attending a Tennessee Titans football game at the Coliseum. The view is from the Nashville Landing adjacent to Riverfront Park. The landing provides a downtown docking facility for all kinds of pleasure craft.*

▼ **Ellington Agriculture Center:** *This cabin and the outdoor utensils are authentic. The iron kettle was once used to wash clothes in boiling water with homemade lye soap as well as to render lard. Regular demonstrations of early farm life are conducted at the center on weekends throughout the summer.*

▲ **The Parthenon:** *The centerpiece of Centennial Park was originally built as a temporary structure for the 1897 Tennessee Centennial Exposition. The first replica of the famous Greek monument stood for twenty-four years after the exposition closed and was replaced by this permanent structure in 1924. Nashville's many classically styled buildings, and particularly the Parthenon, explain why the city is sometimes referred to as "The Athens of the South." Today, the Parthenon's art gallery is home to the Cowan Collection, which includes original American works by artists such as Albert Bierstadt, Winslow Homer, and Frederic Edwin Church.*

In 1778, James Robertson of the Watauga Settlement in North Carolina led a scouting party of eight men to the bluffs overlooking the Cumberland River. He returned the next year with a party of about 250 settlers, made up of men and boys. Robertson's group traveled overland, crossing the mountains through the Cumberland Gap on foot and horseback over Indian and game trails. They arrived on Christmas Day 1779, crossed the frozen Cumberland River, and set about building a fortified station, which they named Fort Nashborough in honor of General Frances Nash, under whom Robertson had served in the American Revolution. A second party, led by Colonel John Donelson, brought another 100 settlers, including women and children as well as thirty-seven slaves in a flotilla of flatboats. Donelson's party arrived on April 24, 1780, after a voyage of 1,100 miles, braving treacherous

shoals and hostile natives. In 1780, the Cumberland Compact was drawn up and signed by 256 men, establishing law in the west. With the end of the Revolutionary War in 1783 the North Carolina legislature created Davidson County, and the following year that same legislature passed an act to establish the town of Nashville. Settlers began leaving the stockade on the river and started building houses and establishing businesses. Merchants, land speculators, and tradesmen all set up shop in Nashville.

The little settlement on the bluffs of the Cumberland River grew rapidly into a thriving frontier community. The first school was established

▲ **Union Station Hotel:** *Opened in 1900 for the L&N and the N.C. & St. L railroads, this grand old station fell upon hard times with the passing of the great age of rail. Fortunately, the Richardson Romanesque structure was completely restored in 1998 and the building transformed into a hotel. The lobby has a sixty-five-foot vaulted ceiling of Tiffany stained glass, gold leaf mirrors, and bas-relief sculptures. Union Station is now a superb Wyndom Historic Hotel with four restaurants and all the amenities of a top-class modern hotel.*

and chartered in 1785, in a log cabin near the site of the present day courthouse. By 1787 property taxes were levied at the rate of one dollar per acre. In 1788, Andrew Jackson, a young lawyer from North Carolina, was appointed attorney general to the Mero district, which is now Middle Tennessee, and settled in Nashville. Tennessee became the sixteenth state admitted into the Union in 1796, a mere sixteen years after the arrival of the Robertson and Donelson parties. Nashville's official status as a city came in 1806 when it was incorporated and a mayor and six aldermen were elected to office.

More settlers were now arriving from the east and north on a network of trails and crude wagon roads. Travel to the west was by river. Goods shipped from Nashville to the port of Natchez, Mississippi, near New Orleans were carried aboard flatboats downstream on the Cumberland to the Tennessee River, then to the Ohio, and on to the Mississippi. The cargo was unloaded in Natchez, the boats were sold for lumber and the crews returned by foot and horseback some 500 miles on the Natchez Trace. The round trip was fraught with danger in both directions, especially from Indians, treacherous water, and highwaymen on the "Trace."

Such perilous travel ended after 1818 with the arrival of the first steamboat in Nashville, the *General Jackson*. It was now possible to travel the waterways in both directions and in the safety and comfort of a larger vessel. Commercial river traffic continues to this day; barges loaded with sand, gravel, and coal are a common sight, while riverboats such as the *Delta Queen*, the *Mississippi Queen*, and the *General Jackson* (a paddle-wheel showboat named for the original) still cruise the Cumberland. Nowadays the Trace is a two-lane scenic highway stretching from Nashville to Natchez, maintained by the National Park Service. The Natchez Trace Parkway begins, or ends depending on one's perspective, in the community of Pasquo at U.S. Highway 100, about fifteen miles west of Downtown.

◄ **Curb Records:** *This recording studio at the corner of Music Square East and Chet Atkins Place is one of several Music Row buildings occupied by Curb Records. During its history, Curb's achievements include 178 number-one singles on the* Billboard *chart, along with seventy number-one albums.*

Nashville was selected as the permanent capital of Tennessee in 1843, and in 1845 work began on a majestic limestone capitol building on Campbell's Hill. William Strickland of Philadelphia was the architect appointed the task of designing and overseeing construction, though unfortunately he died before the building was completed. His remains were entombed in the north wall.

When the Civil War reached the city in 1862, the legislature retreated to Memphis, and Nashville became a Federal city. President Abraham Lincoln appointed Andrew Johnson, of East Tennessee, Military Governor. The capitol building was garrisoned by Union troops and was referred to by the people of the city as Fort Johnson. Expecting the Confederates to try to retake the capital, which was a vital supply link to the west, the Federal army built Fort Negley on a hill south of the city. The Battle of Nashville took place on December 14 and 15, 1864, south and west of the city. The Union troops triumphed and Nashville remained in Federal hands. Fort Negley is today a restored historic site and part of the Nashville park system.

Post-war Nashville recovered and prospered. In 1889, the Nashville Railway and Light Company introduced an electric streetcar service, which further encouraged outward growth and the establishment of new neighborhoods on the outskirts of town. A few years later, to celebrate the "New South" as well as Tennessee's centennial, an exposition was planned on an old racetrack two miles west of the courthouse. Due to several delays caused by financing difficulties and a presidential election, the exposition opened a year late, in 1897. Its centerpiece was a faithful, albeit temporary, replica of the Greek Parthenon, chosen by civic leaders to represent Nashville as the "Athens of the South," because of the numerous colleges in the area. The exposition grounds now form Centennial Park, which boasts a permanent replica of the Parthenon.

The new century dawned in Nashville with the opening of Union Station on Broadway, ten blocks from the riverboat landing. By 1900, the city was served by three railroads: the Nashville, Chattanooga and St. Louis (N.C. & St. L), the Louisville and Nashville (L&N), and the

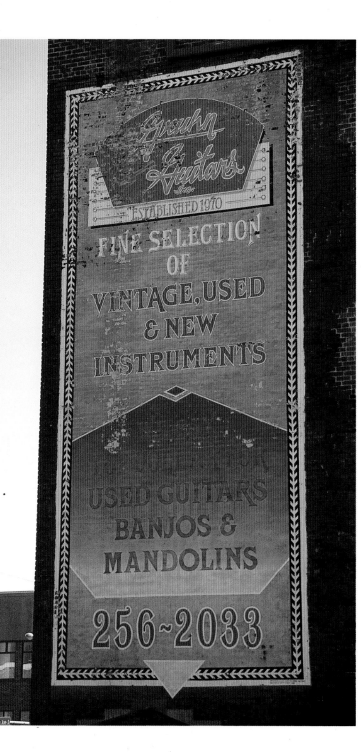

▲ **Gruhn Guitars:** *This renowned store at the corner of Fourth Avenue and Broadway has been selling instruments and repairing vintage guitars and mandolins since 1970. Gruhn's list of regular customers is a virtual who's who of the music world.*

▶ **Legends Corner:** *The ten-foot guitar in front of Legends Corner on "Honky Tonk Row" is one of fifty giant guitars donated by the Gibson Guitar Company and decorated by various Nashville artists for "Guitar Town," a fund-raising arts project for medical research. The theme of this guitar is "honky tonk heroes."*

Tennessee Central. Just twenty years later the railroads had all but replaced steamboats in moving goods and people. Today, Union Station has been transformed into a first-class hotel, and it remains a much-loved Nashville landmark.

Rail wasn't the only change seen in the early twentieth century—during the 1920s the seeds of Nashville's musical reputation were being sown. In 1925, radio station WSM produced the WSM Barn Dance, a program of old-time fiddle music. By 1927 the program's name had been changed to "The Grand Ole Opry" and music was performed before a live audience at several locations around the city. In 1943, The Grand Ole Opry moved into the Ryman Auditorium, where it remained until 1974 when it relocated to its present home, The Grand Ole Opry House, in the Opryland complex east of Downtown. Today, the program is the longest running national show in the United States.

Nashville's celebrated recording industry can be dated back to 1943 when three engineers from WSM founded Castle Recording Studio in the Tulane Hotel. However, Nashville's modern era of recording and the "Nashville Sound" really began in 1954 when Owen Bradley and his brother, Harold, built a studio in a Quonset hut on Sixteenth Avenue. The studio was a roaring success. Soon Sixteenth Avenue became known as "Music Row" as more and more record companies located into the neighborhood to get a piece of the action. Today, Music Row is made up of several streets known as "Music Square." This area is now the home of recording studios, music publishers, booking agencies, and many other music-related businesses, which occupy a curious mixture of towering glass and concrete buildings and quaint old houses.

Modern Nashville is an exciting and vibrant city that retains the charm of the Old South and the manners of a small town while taking a dynamic place in the modern world. Proud of its heritage, its people, and their achievements over the centuries, Nashville is a friendly place where people on the street speak to complete strangers and the final words visitors are likely to hear are "Y'all come back to see us."

Downtown

Downtown Nashville is loosely defined as the area from the Cumberland River west to Twelfth Avenue, and between Jefferson and Lafayette Streets north to south. Within the confines of that area beats the heart of not only the city, but the state of Tennessee. The mayor's office and the city council chambers are both housed in a refurbished Art Deco courthouse in the center of Downtown.

Nashville is enjoying a renaissance as the city continues to grow and change from a retail center to a business, government, and entertainment center. Office towers, apartment buildings, and condominiums spring up almost overnight and older spaces are being renovated into "loft" residences. Specialty shops and restaurants open onto wide, tree-lined sidewalks with flower planters and traffic signals that "chirp" to let pedestrians know in a friendly way that it's safe to cross the street.

The Tennessee State Capitol Building, housing the offices of the Governor, and Secretary of State, and the chambers of the state's House of Representatives and the Senate, sits proudly atop Capitol Hill. It is flanked on the west by the State Library and Archives and the Tennessee Supreme Court buildings, and on the east by the Cordell Hull and the John Sevier state office buildings. The north side of the Capitol looks out over the Bicentennial Capitol Mall State Park. Completing the Capitol Hill complex to the south are the Rachel Jackson Building, the War Memorial Building, and the James K. Polk Building, the latter housing the Tennessee State Museum and the Tennessee Performing Arts Center. War Memorial Plaza sits park-like in the middle. Featuring reflecting pools and fountains, it's a favorite noontime spot for people who work Downtown. It is also used for special events such as The Southern Festival of Books. Self-guided walking tours, with stops indicated by silhouette figures at points of interest, wind through Downtown's street and alleys.

South, down Capitol Boulevard to Church Street stands the 300,000-square-foot main branch of the Nashville Public Library. The library opened on Church Street in 2001, with over 600,000 volumes and room for one million. The library's 4,500-square-foot reading room on the second floor provides the best view in town of Capitol Hill. In addition to the reading room, the library has an enclosed courtyard, an auditorium, a restaurant, and the Nashville Room, an archive of local history.

South of the library on Broadway, ten blocks west of the riverfront, stands the Frist Center of Visual Arts and Union Station Hotel. The building that houses the Frist was completed in 1934 as the main Post Office. When the Post Office moved to larger quarters near Nashville International Airport, the building was converted to an art gallery. Union Station opened in 1900 and served as a rail depot until 1978. It was renovated in1982.

East of the Frist and Union Station Hotel, one block from Broadway, is the Ryman Auditorium. Known as the "Mother Church of Country Music," the Ryman was the home of the Grand Ole Opry from 1943 until 1974. Originally the Ryman was a church, the Union Gospel Tabernacle, completed in 1892 by the Reverend Sam Jones with financial aid from wealthy steamboat captain Tom Ryman. The acoustically superior hall is a regular venue for live performances. The list of speakers and performers who have graced the stage ranges from Sarah Bernhardt, Enrico Caruso, and Charlie Chaplin to Bruce Springstein, Neil Young, Johnny Cash, Hank Williams, and Patsy Cline. A striking bronze statue of Captain Ryman at the wheel of his steamboat stands at the entrance on Fourth Avenue.

▶ **Ryman Auditorium:** *Known as the "Mother Church of Country Music," the auditorium was completed in 1892 as the Union Gospel Tabernacle with financial assistance from steamboat captain Tom Ryman, for whom it is named. From 1943 until 1974 it was the home of the Grand Ole Opry. The Ryman has since been completely renovated and now boasts the new entrance and lobby shown here.*

◀ Answer Bell: *This landmark stands on the northwest corner of the Capitol grounds, facing Bicentennial Capitol Mall State Park. The bell rings in answer to the ninety-five-bell carillon in the Court of Three Stars in the park. The ninety-five bells represent the ninety-five counties in Tennessee.*

▲ Tennessee State Capitol Building: *Construction on the building was completed in 1859 and has undergone two major renovations. The interior was refurbished and the columns replaced in 1955, and the interior was returned to its 1850s splendor in 2004. The Capitol Building was designed by Philadelphia architect William Strickland, who died in 1854 before the building was completed and is entombed in the north wall.*

▶ Alvin C. York Statue: *York was a young man in rural Pall Mall, Tennessee, in the Cumberland Mountains, when the United States entered World War I. On receiving his draft notice he tried to register with the board as a conscientious objector. Despite this initial reluctance to go to war, Sergeant York went on to win the United States highest award for a soldier, the Medal of Honor.*

ALVIN C. YORK
ARMED WITH HIS RIFLE AND PISTOL, HIS COURAGE AND SKILL, THIS ONE TENNESSEAN
SILENCED A GERMAN BATTALION OF 35 MACHINE GUNS, KILLING 25 ENEMY SOLDIERS AND
CAPTURING 132 IN THE ARGONNE FOREST OF FRANCE OCTOBER 1918

President James K. Polk Tomb: *President Polk died in 1849 and was buried in this mausoleum on the grounds of Polk Place, his home on Vine Street (now Seventh Avenue). The home was sold after the death of Mrs. Polk and the remains of both the president and his wife were moved to the northeast corner of the Capitol grounds.*

Andrew Jackson Statue at Night: *The State Capitol Building silhouettes the statue of General Jackson on horseback. The pose represents a military officer, his horse rearing while he lifts his chapeau to salute the troops in review.*

Andrew Jackson Statue: *Situated on the east side of the Capitol Building, the statue was cast in triplicate and dedicated in 1880. Its two siblings were placed on the grounds of the White House in Washington, D.C., and in Jackson Square, New Orleans. The sculptor, Clark Mills, described it as "the first equestrian statue ever self posed on the hind feet in the world."*

◀◀ **War Memorial Plaza:** *Directly in front of the Capitol Building, the plaza is a favorite gathering place for lunching Downtown workers, and hosts various special events including political rallies and The Southern Festival Of Books.*

◀ **Southeast from the Capitol:** *Across War Memorial Plaza are the Rachel Jackson Building and the James K. Polk Office Building, which houses the Tennessee State Museum and The Tennessee Performing Arts Center. To the right are the City Center and the Hermitage Hotel. The bronze statue overlooking Downtown is of Edward Ward Carmack, a newspaperman and civic leader of the late 1800s.*

▲ **Tennessee Performing Arts Center:** *Referred to locally as TPAC (Teepak), the center is home to the Nashville Ballet Company, the Nashville Opera Association, the Tennessee Repertory Theater, and touring Broadway companies. A total of three auditoriums have a combined seating of 3,803. The Nashville Symphony Orchestra, which used to reside here, moved into a new Symphony Hall in 2006.*

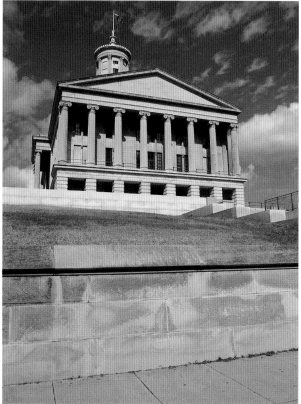

◀ **Capitol Building Reliquary:** *On the north lawn of the Capitol is a monument to the 1850s stonecutters, carvers, and masons who helped to build the Capitol. These pieces, placed here in 1996, are remnants of the original Greek ionic columns that were replaced due to deterioration in 1955.*

▲ **Capitol Building Limestone:** *The stone used to build the retaining wall that surrounds the Capitol grounds, as well as the Capitol Building, was quarried a short distance from the site. Close examination reveals marks made by the hand tools used at that time. Many of the stone carvers and masons who worked on the construction were immigrants from Germany.*

▲ **Nashville Public
Library:** *Nashville's recent
addition to the citywide
library system is the
300,000-square-foot, $85-
million, Downtown Library,*

*which opened in 2001. The
grand 4,500-square-foot
reading room seen here
overlooks Capitol Boulevard
and the State Capitol.*

Nash Trash Tours: *Run by a unique Nashville tour company, the most entertaining way to see the city is by Nash Trash bus. Billed as "the wackiest tour in Nashville," a Nash Trash tour is a two-act comedy in a bright pink bus.*

The Frist Center For The Visual Arts: *Located between Ninth and Tenth Avenues on Broadway, this Art Deco building originally opened in 1934 as the Downtown main Post Office. It was renovated and reopened as an art gallery in 2000. The Frist Center's art exhibits range from paintings by old masters to folk art and contemporary works, while programs of chamber music can be heard inside the building and jazz musicians perform in the back courtyard.*

The Hermitage Hotel: *This is the best Beaux Arts commercial building still in use in Nashville. The Hermitage Hotel opened on the corner of Union Street and Sixth Avenue in 1910 and was the city's first million-dollar hotel. It has been completely renovated and updated at a cost of seventeen million dollars and is now one of the finest luxury hotels in Tennessee.*

◄ **Shelby Street Bridge:**
*The bridge was in constant
use from its completion in
1907 until 1998 when it was
found to be unsafe for heavy
vehicle traffic. A new bridge
was constructed for vehicles,
and Shelby Street Bridge was
rebuilt as a pedestrian bridge
linking the Riverfront with the
Coliseum on the east bank.*

▲ **Shelby Street Bridge
Observation Deck:** *This
deck is one of four, two to
each side of the bridge,
decorated with a riverboat
theme on the sides and
wood pavers. The bridge is
accessible from the
Downtown side by a glass-
enclosed elevator and is a
popular route for joggers,
cyclists, and walkers.*

Broadway

Broadway begins at the Cumberland River near the site of the old Nashville Wharf and runs directly west to Twenty-First Avenue. The city's first wholesale district, it was originally named Broad Street because that is exactly what it was—a very broad, flat, dirt street, wide enough to allow teamsters to maneuver large wagons.

One of the oldest buildings still in use on Broadway predates the Civil War. It once housed William Stockell's concrete and plaster business; then during the Civil War the Union Army used it as a hospital. Today, it is the home of the Ernest Tubb Record Shop, which has been at that location since 1947. It was in the latter part of the nineteenth century that the multi-story brick buildings with elaborate facades and sidewalks were built on both sides of the street from Front Street at the river to about present day Sixth Avenue. Fortunately, many of these buildings have survived the decades and still give the area its unique character, even if they now house businesses that the original owners could not have imagined.

On the north side of Broadway between Second and Fifth Avenues stands a row of narrow two- and three-story buildings, which were once stores, shops, and offices. Today, the buildings are known collectively as "Honky Tonk Row" and are the starting place for many ambitious young singers and musicians. The origin of the phrase "honky tonk" is unknown, but *Webster's Encyclopedic Dictionary* defines it as meaning "a cheap night club or dance-hall." What was once a derogatory term is now a quaint description of these colorful businesses. Tootsies Orchid Lounge is the most well-known, and the most colorful. It was named by owner Tootsie Best after a contractor painted the outside of the building a bright orchid color. All day and into the night the sounds of country music, performed live on stage, pour from its open doors as well as from those of its neighbors—The Bluegrass Inn, Robert's Western World, The Stage, and Legends Corner.

Nashville's musical tradition is also to be found at Gruhn Guitars, with its 3,000-square-foot showroom of vintage and new instruments, situated at the corner of Fourth Avenue and Broadway. The Country Music Hall of Fame and Museum is located one block south of Broadway on Demonbreun Street between Fourth and Fifth Avenues. However, country music is not the only thing to give Broadway its flavor. The unmistakable aroma of hickory-smoked barbeque from Jacks Bar-B-Que on the north side and Rippy's on the south is a fragrant reminder of what part of the world you are in.

Also at Fifth and Broadway, on the southwest corner, stands the Gaylord Entertainment Center, home to the Nashville Predators NHL Hockey Team, the CMA Music Fest, and host to innumerable major concerts. The Nashville Convention Center is at the northwest corner on the opposite side of Broadway, while one of the largest souvenir shops in the city is located at the corner of Second Avenue and Broadway. Cotton-Eyed Joe's, named for a very old country square-dance song, sells everything from western hats to salt shakers shaped like outhouses. On the south side of Broadway are new entertainment businesses such as The Red Iguana, WannaB's Karaoke Bar, and several up-scale restaurants. The Hard Rock Café takes up one block of Broadway from Second to First Avenue. The café is in a renovated nineteenth century commercial building and the gift shop is housed in what was originally a saloon.

▶ **Tootsies Orchid Lounge:** *This "World Famous" spot was a favorite watering hole for Grand Ole Opry performers in the 1960s and 70s, before the "Opry" moved out of the Ryman. Several country hits were written on the back of paper napkins in Tootsies.*

◄ **Honky Tonk Row:**
On the north side of
Broadway between Fourth
and Fifth Avenues is the
famous Honky Tonk Row.
Passers-by are enticed inside
these great old dance halls
by the sounds of music from
the stage and aromas from
the kitchen.

▲ **Bluegrass Inn:** *Bill
Monroe named his unique
style of hard driving music
"bluegrass," for his home
state of Kentucky. He
introduced it to the world on
the stage of the Grand Ole
Opry, across the alley from
Honky Tonk Row. You can still
hear bluegrass at the Ryman
as well as nightly at the
Bluegrass Inn.*

◀ **Broadway Marker:**
*This inlayed marker, at the
corner of Broadway and
Second Avenue, is set into
the pavement in front of the
Hard Rock Café gift shop.*

▼ **Cotton-Eyed Joe's:**
At the corner of Broadway
and Second Avenue, opposite
the Hard Rock Café, Cotton-
Eyed Joe's is the largest, and
certainly the most visible,

souvenir shop in Nashville. On
three floors it sells everything
from the western hats seen
below left to country-themed
décor items.

Hatch Show Print: *Amazingly preserved, Hatch's has been producing event posters since 1879, and still uses the same techniques and equipment to print reproductions of original posters as well as new designs. The oldest-known letterpress poster shop in the United States, Hatch is now owned and operated by the Country Music Hall Of Fame and Museum.*

Ernest Tubb Record Shop: *This is the most recognizable sign on Broadway. Country music legend Ernest Tubb, who billed himself as the "Texas Troubadour," opened his record shop in 1947. He also held the Midnight Jamboree at this location on Saturday nights. Today, it is held at the Texas Troubadour Theatre near Opryland.*

Gruhn Guitars: *One of several showrooms at Gruhn Guitars on Broadway, this room is devoted to acoustic instruments. Guitars at Gruhn's range in price from a few hundred to several thousand dollars and include instruments once owned by some of the best-known musicians in the world.*

◀ **Historic District Carriage:** *The best way to see the Historic District is from a carriage drawn by a good team of horses, with a cowgirl at the reins, of course.*

▶ **Hard Rock Café:** *The Nashville premises of the world-famous Hard Rock Café take up the entire block from Second to First Avenues at the end of Broadway. The previous business in this building was a wholesale hardware company, and the unusual sign on the wall originally advertised Moore Paints. The "Moore man" has become a local landmark.*

▶ **Country Music Hall of Fame and Museum:** *Located on Demonbreun Street one block south of Broadway between Fourth and Fifth Avenues, the museum is a repository of rare country music artifacts. The Hall of Fame often hosts special events, while the museum collection includes 600 instruments, 800 stage costumes, and a library of music, recordings, and country music treasures.*

▲ **Gaylord
Entertainment Center:**
*At the corner of Fifth Avenue
and Broadway, the Gaylord
Entertainment Center is
home to NHL hockey team
the Nashville Predators, a
convention exhibit hall, and a
concert venue. Since 1996,
the center has hosted
numerous country, rock, and
classical concerts as well as
the CMA Music Fest. It is
connected to the Nashville
Convention Center across
Broadway.*

▶ **Radio Show at the
Gaylord:** *Local radio
stations frequently stage
events such as this one in
front of the Gaylord
Entertainment Center, which
is also referred to locally as
"the arena." This view is from
the rooftop seating area of
Rippy's Smokin' Bar & Grill.*

◀ **The Nashville Convention Center:** *The Convention Center is connected to both the Gaylord Entertainment Center and the Renaissance Hotel. It boasts 118,675-square-feet of exhibit space, twenty-five meeting rooms, and a grand ballroom. Delegates will find that it is only a short walk from here to the entertainment spots, bars, and restaurants of Broadway and Second Avenue.*

▶ **WannaB's Karaoke Bar:** *These Harley-Davidson motorcycles are parked in front of WannaB's and the Red Iguana on the south side of Broadway. Several restaurants and clubs on the south side offer alternatives to country music.*

◀ **Joe's Crab Shack:** *This favorite spot for locals and tourists alike is a tropical-themed seafood restaurant on the southwestern corner of Broadway and Second Avenue. The interior is designed to resemble a Gulf Coast fishing camp.*

Market Street

Second Avenue is the only street in Nashville commonly referred to by its historic name, Market Street, which citizens still cling to nearly a century after all the north to south cross-streets in the city were renamed to make finding addresses easier. Today, Market Street is lined on both sides with nineteenth-century brick buildings that once housed wholesale businesses, a laundry, barbershops, and saloons. Restaurants, nightclubs, a dinner theater, and specialty shops occupy these handsome old structures now. First and Second Avenues as well as Broadway and the Riverfront make up "The District," an unofficial title given to this historic section of the city along the riverfront. The area hosts many cultural and entertainment events including concerts held on a floating stage at River Front Park, and Dancing in the District, a weekly draw for thousands of blues, jazz, and rock fans.

All the buildings on the east side of Second Avenue are narrow and long and open in the rear onto First Avenue, which was Front Street in the old days of steamboats. Thus stevedores with their teams of mules only had to move goods a few yards to the warehouses from boats tied up at the Nashville wharf. On the west side, across the street from the Hard Rock Café, is the Jack Daniel's Store where you can buy everything related to Jack Daniel's, except the product itself. However, the thirsty shopper can visit the nearby Mulligan's Irish Pub. Miss Marple's Mystery Dinner Theater is also located on the west side for those who like their meals accompanied by entertainment.

One of the most notable of the original businesses on Market Street was a retail liquor store owned by George A. Dickel, who also operated the Silver Dollar Saloon on the corner of Market and Broad Streets, with his brother-in-law. Back then the Silver Dollar was considered a fancy place due, in part, to the silver dollars inlaid into the floor and the suspended gas burner next to the glass tobacco case, which was provided for cigar-puffing customers. Fortunately, a little piece of this heritage has been preserved. The Silver Dollar is now the gift shop for the Hard Rock Café, but a small section of the floor, with its silver dollars, has been restored.

A more recent addition to Second Avenue is the Wild Horse Saloon, a multi-level dance hall housed in a new building that was designed to co-habit harmoniously with its historic neighbors. There is more to the music scene in Nashville than country on Second Avenue; blues, jazz, and contemporary music clubs nestle comfortably among the country bars.

▶ **Market Street Brewery and Public House:** *A great microbrewery with a menu of English and American favorites, the Market Street Brewery's wood-paneled interior is warm and cozy, and the view of the river from the back tables is one of the best in the district.*

◀▲ **Wild Horse Saloon:** *A multi-level, 66,000-square-foot restaurant, bar, dance hall, and concert venue, the Wild Horse opened in 1996. Since then it has been the scene of over 4,000 television and music video tapings. The wild horse itself greets fans coming to the saloon, which is one of the largest in Tennessee. In a given year the kitchen uses close to 3,000 gallons of barbeque sauce and around two million pickles for the house specialty, fried pickles.*

▶ **Wild Horse Guitar:** *Sarah Evans, multi-platinum recording star, was the inspiration for the ten-foot guitar in front of the Wild Horse Saloon.*

▲ **Dancing at the Wild Horse:** *More than one and a half million country music fans visit the Wild Horse annually. Many of them, like the ones seen here, take advantage of the large dance floor and free lessons. Major stars who have performed on this stage include Reba McEntire, Andy Griggs, Ronnie Milsap, Trace Atkins, and Sugarland.*

▶ **Butler's Run:** *This covered walkway runs between two buildings from Second to First Avenues. The monument seen here is to the memory of the dog for whom the walkway was named. The inscription on the pedestal tells Butler's story.*

BUTLER, A BEAUTIFUL COMBINATION OF SPRINGER SPANIEL AND BLACK LABRADOR RETRIEVER, WAS ADOPTED IN 1990 FROM THE NASHVILLE HUMANE SOCIETY BY THE BUILDING'S OWNERS. HE DEDICATED THIS ALLEYWAY AT THE THRESHOLD WITH HIS PAW PRINT AND EARNED THE TITLE, THE "CANINE BON VIVANT" AT THE MANY CIVIC AND SOCIAL FUNCTIONS IN THE UPPER LEVEL RESIDENCE. BUTLER, THROUGH HIS DAILY DOWNTOWN WALKS, BECAME ONE OF THE MOST WELL KNOWN CANINE CITIZENS OF NASHVILLE. HE DIED ON OCTOBER 7, 1999, AND ALTHOUGH THIS PASSAGEWAY TO THE RIVER IS FOR PEOPLE, IT WILL ALWAYS BE

BUTLER'S RUN

▲ **Charlie Daniels Museum and Gift Shop:** *Charlie Daniels is one of the best loved of Nashville's musicians, with a career spanning country and honky tonk to gospel. He is known for his patriotism as well as his music, as is evident in the decoration on the giant guitar in front of the premises. Inside can be found memorabilia and artifacts spanning the artist's great touring history. The Wild Horse Saloon and the Hard Rock Café flank the museum on either side.*

▶ **B. B. King's Blues Club:** *This is the place to go on Second Avenue for live "Memphis" blues music and traditional Southern food. The excellent menu ranges from Memphis-style ribs and barbeque pork to Southern fried catfish and seafood gumbo.*

North Nashville

Historically, North Nashville comprised the area directly north of the Capitol Building, over Jefferson Street, to the community of Bordeaux across the Cumberland River. Today, the northern part of Nashville and Davidson County includes Bordeaux, the communities of Joelton, White's Creek, Union Hill, Goodlettsville, Madison, and Old Hickory.

Bicentennial Capitol Mall State Park begins directly north of the Tennessee State Capitol Building and continues to Jefferson Street. Within the boundaries of the park, which is commonly known as Bicentennial Mall, are monuments to the history of Tennessee, including an amphitheater and the Court of Three Stars—a ninety-five bell carillon. The three stars represent the three grand divisions of Tennessee and can also be found on the state flag. The number of bells represents the ninety-five counties of the state.

Flanking Bicentennial Mall is the Nashville Farmers' Market, where farmers and nursery workers from middle Tennessee, northern Alabama, and southern Kentucky sell seasonal produce and landscape plants. Multinational and regional cuisine is served up to visitors by vendors in the food court.

To the north of Jefferson Street is a small neighborhood known as Germantown, which was settled in the nineteenth century by immigrants, most of whom—as the area's name suggests—hailed from Germany. A large number of the new citizens found work in the meat processing industry that was a major part of the city's economy until the 1960s, when the plants along the river closed. This caused an inevitable slump in the district's fortunes for a while, but Germantown is now enjoying a revival. Many of the old townhouses and cottages are being restored and new, period-style homes are being built.

Across the Cumberland River, which runs a serpentine course through the city, the more outlying northern section of Nashville retains much of its original rural flavor. Farms, forested hills, and grassy meadows dominate the landscape. Beaman Park, the city's newest nature park, is located in northwestern Davison County on the Highland Rim. Accessible from Eaton's Creek Road, the park is a 1,500-acre mixed hardwood forest with a diverse population of wildlife. Deer, wild turkey, songbirds, and hundreds of species of wildflowers can be found in this natural treasure.

The community of Goodlettsville straddles the Davidson-Sumner County line. Kasper Mansker built a fort, or "station," here in 1780 along the creek that now bears his name, and a faithful reproduction of Mansker's Station has been built on the banks of Mansker's Creek in Moss Wright Park. Historic reenactors now demonstrate how the pioneers lived to tourists visiting the fort. Special events are also held regularly. Just as popular, though for very different reasons, is Goodlettsville's Rivergate Mall, a huge retail shopping mall. Along with surrounding stores, it is a major retail center for northern middle Tennessee and southern Kentucky.

▶ **Crocker Springs Bed and Breakfast:** *This beautiful old 1880s farmhouse on Crocker Springs Road, in the community of Goodlettsville, was turned into a bed and breakfast by Jack and Bev Spangler. The couple took great care in preserving the authentic look and feel of a nineteenth-century, middle Tennessee farm—the front porch was even repaired using posts and trim from Melrose, a historic house that once stood in south Nashville.*

▶ **Bicentennial Capitol Mall State Park:** *Dedicated in 1996, the park is commonly referred to simply as Bicentennial Mall. This section of its nineteen acres is the Court of Three Stars, encircled by a ninety-five bell carillon. The three stars represent the three grand divisions of Tennessee and the carillon represents the ninety-five counties of the state. The park is close to the site of the first settlement in the area—French Lick, a 1700s fur trading station.*

▶ **Baptist Sports Park:** *The practice facility for the Tennessee Titans NFL football team is in Metro Center. The 80,000-square-foot building contains weight rooms, meeting rooms, coaches' and administrative offices, as well as an auditorium. There are three practice fields; two outdoors and one under cover. The outdoor fields are oriented the same direction to the sun as the Coliseum.*

▶ **Millennium Maxwell House Hotel:**

Five minutes north of Downtown, adjacent to Metro Center, is this landmark hotel. It was named for Nashville's original Maxwell House Hotel, which was destroyed by fire in 1961. Today's guests are greeted by soft country music and a complimentary GooGoo candy bar, a local delicacy made by Nashville's Standard Candy Company since 1912.

▲ **Beaman Park:**
Northwest of Downtown on the edge of the Highland Rim, Nashville's newest nature park is a 1,500-acre hardwood forest adjacent to Eaton's Creek. Hiking trails wind through woodland that is rich in native plants and wildflowers. This photograph shows the Highland Trailhead with access to the Ridgetop Trail and Henry Hollow Loop.

▶ A Cowboy Town: *Milk cans and a wagon wheel become works of art at A Cowboy Town, an Old West themed corporate retreat in the community of White's Creek.*

▶ Historic Mansker's Station Frontier Life Center: *In Goodlettsville is an authentic reproduction of Kasper Mansker's 1780 fort and a fascinating glimpse into the early days of Nashville's colonial past. Reenactors in authentic dress conduct living history demonstrations and hold special events throughout the year. An annual Colonial Trade Faire is also held for two days every May.*

South Nashville

Beginning on the south side of Broadway, Downtown, and continuing to Williamson County, southern Nashville is where you will find the State Fairgrounds, the Old City Cemetery, and the communities of Woodbine, Antioch, Berry Hill, Green Hills, and Oak Hill. It is also home to Music Row, which begins at the junction of Sixteenth Avenue, Division, and Demonbreum Streets at Nashville's only roundabout intersection. Most of the businesses at the heart of the city's legendary recording industry can be found between Sixteenth and Nineteenth Avenues and south from Division Street to Wedgewood Avenue.

Co-existing peacefully with the music corporations is the rather more scholarly Belmont University. The campus faces Wedgewood Avenue and is also the site of Belmont Mansion, built as a summer home by Adelicia Acklen and completed in 1853. Not far away is another historic Nashville home. Travellers Rest, which lies just east of Franklin Pike, was built in the style of a Virginia farmhouse at a time when most houses in the area were log structures. It was constructed in 1798 by Judge John Overton, who was at one time the law partner of Andrew Jackson, the area's first attorney general. Today, Travellers Rest is preserved as a museum and is fortunate to be under the care of the Colonial Dames of America.

More rural treasures to the south of Nashville include the beautiful Radnor Lake State Natural Area and Ellington Agriculture Center. Radnor Lake is on Otter Creek Road at the southwestern edge of the Nashville, between Franklin Pike and Granny White Pike. The eighty-five-acre lake was originally created in 1924 to provide water to the Radnor railroad yards a few miles to the east. However, the state purchased it along with 747 surrounding acres in 1974, and it is now maintained by the Tennessee Department of State Parks. The Ellington Agriculture Center is a short distance east of Radnor Lake at the end of Hogan Road and has a noble equestrian history. The property and mansion once comprised Brentwood Stables, a thoroughbred horse farm, but today are home to the Tennessee Department of Agriculture and the Tennessee Wildlife Resources Agency. The Tennessee Agricultural Museum is housed in a renovated plantation barn on the property. In keeping with its heritage, horses still graze in the rolling hills of the complex, because the mounted division of the Metropolitan Nashville Police Department stables its animals here.

Further east again is Grassmere, another old Nashville house, once the ancestral residence of sisters Elise and Margaret Croft and now home to the Nashville Zoo. The zoo has preserved the past carefully and offers guided tours of the Grassmere Historic Farm.

Another of Nashville's wonderful parks is located at the Davidson-Rutherford County line, along the eastern shore of J. Percy Priest Lake, a U.S. Army Corps of Engineers impoundment on the Stones River. Long Hunter State Park was named for the early explorers of the area and is a 2,657-acre park complete with twenty-eight miles of hiking trails, a 110-acre lake, and a unique hardwood cedar forest. It is also the site of an annual three-day Pow Wow held by the Native American Indian Association of Tennessee.

▶ **Ellington Agriculture Center:** *The campus-like compound of offices and laboratories housing the Tennessee Department of Agriculture and the Tennessee Wildlife Resources Agency is named for Buford Ellington, a commissioner of agriculture and a Tennessee governor. This wagon sits outside the Oscar L. Farris Agriculture Museum on the grounds.*

▶ **American Society of Composers, Authors, and Publishers:** *On the corner of Music Square West and Broadway Avenue are the local offices of this powerful music licensing association. With many household names among its 225,000 members, ASCAP protects the rights of composers, songwriters, music publishers, and lyricists.*

◀ **Sony Music Group:** *The Nashville offices of one of the world's largest record labels are in an innocuous-looking modern building on Music Square West, marked by an Elvis-themed guitar outside. In the early years of Music Row most of the music businesses were in old houses converted to offices, but as the industry grew, many companies have opted for contemporary buildings, specifically designed to accommodate large workforces and all the technology they need.*

▶ **RCA Studio B Museum:** *This simple building on Seventeenth Avenue is the legendary RCA Studio B, now managed as a museum by the Country Music Hall of Fame and one of the most popular stops on tours of Music Row. During the 1970s Elvis Presley, Roy Orbison, Chet Atkins, the Everly Brothers, and Dolly Parton all recorded here.*

▷ **Island Bound Music:**
On Seventeenth Avenue is a company typical of the music businesses that have transformed this neighborhood into Music Row. Behind the doors of these converted historic houses, some of the world's best-known songs have been written or recorded. The availability of "A list" studio musicians, producers, engineers, and songwriters has helped put Nashville on the world's music map.

◀ **Fort Negley:** *Built by the Union Army in 1862 to defend occupied Nashville from a Confederate attack to the south, the fort became an overgrown ruin after the war. Many of its stones were even used to build the city reservoir a short distance away on Franklin Pike (now Eighth Avenue South).*

▶ **William Driver Memorial:** *Driver, a sea captain from Salem, Massachusetts, retired to Nashville in 1837. He brought with him his flag, which he had named Old Glory. The flag later found fame after it was raised over the Capitol when the Union Army took over the city. Captain Driver's flag is now on display in the Smithsonian Museum of American History in Washington, D.C., but Captain Driver is buried here, in the Old City Cemetery, on Fourth Avenue South near Lafayette Street.*

◀ **Fort Negley:** *Happily, Fort Negley was restored and opened as a museum site by Metro Parks in 2004. It is now a popular tourist destination and offers spectacular views of Nashville.*

◄ State Fairgrounds, Midway: *Every September the Midway, seen here, comes alive at dusk with rides and games—the most exciting part of the weeklong fair that has been held on these grounds on Fourth Avenue South since 1908. The fairgrounds are also used for special events and stock car races all year round.*

▲ State Fairgrounds, Music City Motorplex: *Originally a dirt track used for harness racing, the raceway is now a paved, banked ⅝-mile oval track. Built in 1957, it also has a smaller ¼-mile oval inside. The Motorplex hosts Saturday night racing. Stock car racing is the most attended spectator sport in the U.S.*

▼ The Adventure Science Center: *This learning center with changing, interactive exhibits and a permanent planetarium is a popular field trip destination for school children from middle Tennessee, southern Kentucky, and north Alabama. It is located on Fort Negley Boulevard at the foot of St. Cloud Hill.*

▶ **Sunny Side:** *This Federal-style house in Sevier Park was built by Mary Benton in 1843. Mary was the widow of Jessie Benton, once a close associate of Andrew Jackson. The house has been restored and is now the office of the Metro Historical Commission.*

◀ **Belmont Mansion:** *Built between 1849 and 1853 by Joseph and Adelicia Acklen as a summer home, Belmont Mansion and its estate boasted a bowling alley, fountains, an artificial lake, a zoo, and its own refinery to produce gas for lighting. It was originally named "Belle Monte," from the Italian for beautiful mountain. It is now open regularly for tours and is to be found on the Campus of Belmont University.*

▶ **Travellers Rest:** *In 1799 Judge John Overton built Travellers Rest on the site of a vast Native American burial ground in the style of a Virginia farmhouse. Judge Overton served as traveling circuit court judge and referred to himself as the weary "traveler," which is how his home came by its name. Today, Travellers Rest is held in trust by the National Society of the Colonial Dames of America in Tennessee and is open for tours and special events.*

◀ **Dyer Observatory:**
Atop the highest point in southern Davidson County, Vanderbilt University's Dyer Observatory is popular with visiting school children, who can videoconference with astronomy experts and former astronauts here. It is also the site of Music on the Mountain, concerts that range from Appalachian to big band music.

▲ **Travellers Rest, Garden:** *Like the house itself, Mrs. Mary Overton's garden has undergone many changes and additions. During her time here the grounds provided flowers to decorate the table as well as medicinal herbs. The garden is just a few steps from the veranda, or lower gallery.*

▶ **Battle of Nashville Monument:** *On Granny White Pike near Battlefield Drive is a memorial to both Union and Confederate soldiers who died in the Battle of Nashville. It stood on Franklin Pike from 1927, but after a tornado toppled the obelisk in 1974 it was restored and moved to this small park in 1992, closer to the actual site of the battle.*

◀ **Radnor Lake State Natural Area:** *This eighty-five-acre lake on Otter Creek Road was built in 1924 to provide water to the L&N rail yards. Together with the surrounding 773 acres, it was purchased by the State of Tennessee in 1973 and is now a protected natural area maintained by the Tennessee Department of State Parks. Since the purchase it has been enlarged further, and the park now encompasses 1,100 acres with seven miles of trails.*

▶ **Oscar L. Farris Museum:** *Farm implements and equipment on display in the museum range from kitchen utensils and blacksmith tools to the steam-powered tractor seen here. The display also includes a horse drawn buggy that was once used to deliver mail.*

▶ **Oscar L. Farris Museum:** *This photograph shows an original, fully functional loom and a spinning wheel, which are housed upstairs in what was once a hayloft.*

▶ **Oscar L. Farris Museum:** *Housed in this remolded plantation barn, the museum is named for a Davidson County agricultural extension agent who served from 1920 to 1942. When the museum opened in 1957, Farris donated most of the items then on display from his personal collection. He continued to add to the museum's archive until his death in 1961.*

◀ **Ellington Agriculture Center, Music and Molasses Festival:** *Each year, near the end of September, this festival is held on the center's grounds. Featuring two music stages and old-time cooking demonstrations (including molasses making) as well as story-telling, buggy rides, trail hikes, and country cloggers, the festival draws thousands annually. This front-porch stage was the caretaker's house when this property was Brentwood Hall, a sprawling horse farm.*

◀ **Ellington Agriculture Center, Music and Molasses Festival:** *This photograph shows a blacksmith in period clothing demonstrating his trade at the festival. Displays of traditional crafts are a big attraction and a wonderful way to see first-hand how life was once lived around Nashville.*

▶ **Nashville Zoo:** *Located on Nolensville Pike on the grounds of Grassmere, a historic farm six miles south of Downtown, the zoo is designed as a wildlife park that simulates the animals' natural habitats. A field that once pastured cattle has been turned into a savannah for three African elephants.*

▲ **Grassmere:** *Michael Dunn of Virginia built this farmhouse shortly after he purchased the 272 acres around 1810. It was subsequently sold and passed down to family members, and in 1859 it was named Grassmere. Elise and Margaret Croft took possession in 1952 and lived out their lives here before eventually willing the farm to the Cumberland Museum. It is now part of the Nashville Zoo and is open for tours.*

▲ **101st Airborne Restaurant:** *Ten miles from Downtown and next to Nashville International Airport, this restaurant is designed to look like a World War II French farmhouse, with army trucks and jeeps decorating the front lawn. Adding to the authentic appearance is a DC-3 airplane. The interior has working fireplaces, a cozy bar, and is decorated with 1940s photographs and memorabilia. The food is American fare—steaks, seafood, and salads.*

▶ **Long Hunter State Park, Pow Wow and Fall Festival:** *A Native American Indian dancer competes in the sacred circle at this popular annual festival held in Long Hunter State Park on the southern edge of Davidson County. The Native American Indian Association of Tennessee holds the three-day fund-raising event each year.*

East Nashville

Prior to the Civil War, East Nashville and Edgefield were separate towns on the east bank of the Cumberland River. Today, Edgefield is a historic district and East Nashville, with its mix of architectural styles covering several periods, is rapidly being rediscovered and renovated. However, this part of the city was very nearly lost for good in 1916 when a massive fire, fanned by a dry March wind, destroyed 648 East Nashville homes. A large section of the ruined neighborhood is now East Park and is surrounded by restored homes, new houses, and condominiums designed to blend with the existing historic structures. The east side of Nashville also includes Lockland Springs, Inglewood, Donelson, and Hermitage.

Another of Nashville's great parks is Shelby Park, which is to be found just beyond Lockland Springs next to the Cumberland River. It was opened by the city in 1912 and originally comprised 121 acres of land. An additional fifty acres were purchased in 1927 for the city's first municipal golf course, and in 1997, 810 acres of prime wetlands were added to the park with the opening of Shelby Bottoms Greenway and Nature Park. This haven for migrating birds and resident wildlife has five miles of paved walkways and another five miles of primitive trails as well as boardwalks, overlooks on the river bank, and seven rustic bridges.

This part of Nashville also boasts one of the world's most amazing resorts. Opryland Resort and Convention Center is in the community of Donelson, across the Cumberland River from Shelby Bottoms. Among its many attractions, Opryland Hotel has nine acres of indoor gardens, winding rivers with flatboats, a forty-four-foot-high waterfall, and walking paths; all under glass in three climate-controlled atriums. It also has an incredible 2,888 rooms and 60,000 square-feet of meeting space, including the Ryman Exhibit Hall, the largest single-level, self-contained facility in a hotel in the U.S.

The Grand Ole Opry House is part of the Opryland Complex and has been home of the Grand Ole Opry, the nation's longest running radio show, since 1974. Next to the Opry House are the Bell South Acuff Theater and the Grand Ole Opry Museum as well as the *General Jackson* showboat and Opry Mills, a mega mall of specialty stores, theaters, and restaurants. As if this wasn't enough for any tourist, the Gaylord Springs Golf Course is a par seventy-two, eighteen-hole course built along the banks of the Cumberland River in Pennington Bend. Opryland is built on land that was once part of Two Rivers Plantation, the site of the impressive Two Rivers Mansion built in the 1870s. Today, the Mansion, which is situated between the Cumberland River and Stones River, is owned by the Metro Nashville Parks Department.

Andrew Jackson's Hermitage is in the community of Hermitage near the Wilson, Davidson County line. The state of Tennessee purchased the Hermitage from the Jackson family in 1856, and it was entrusted to the Ladies' Hermitage Association in 1889. The mansion and grounds, including the original log house and slave cabins, are open to the public and are now the third most-visited presidential museum in the U.S. Hermitage Church, built by Jackson for his wife Rachel, is just south of the Hermitage at Tulip Grove.

▶ **Gaylord Opryland Hotel and Convention Center:**
The resort is located just across the river and a little north of Shelby Bottoms in the community of Donelson. This photograph shows the Magnolia Lobby entrance to the 2,888-room Opryland Hotel, decked in lights for the holidays.

The Gerst Haus German and American Restaurant: *Named for the Gerst Brewery that was in business from 1890 until the 1950s, this great old eatery has been a favorite with generations of Nashvillians. The restaurant has been forced to relocate twice, the first time for a Downtown urban renewal project, and later to make way for the Coliseum. The menu ranges from traditional German dishes to the Gerst Haus oyster roll specialty.*

Top O' Woodland Bed and Breakfast Inn: *Dr. H.B. Hyde built his home—described as Grand Queen Ann/Neoclassical Victorian—between 1890 and 1904. Much of the interior is original and the house is completely furnished with period pieces. Inside are twelve chandeliers, five fireplaces, solid chestnut pocket doors, and no television! Dr. Hyde's old house, located in Historic Lockland Springs on Woodland Street, now welcomes guests looking for peace and quiet.*

◄ **Coliseum:** *The 61,149-seat Coliseum on the east side of the Cumberland River is home to the Tennessee Titans NFL football team. The facility has two large club lounges with food and beverage service, 1,200 club seats, sixty concession stands, and parking for 7,500 vehicles. It is also the home field for Tennessee State University's football team.*

► **Shelby Bottoms Nature Park:** *This rare urban wetland of 810 acres flanks three miles of the Cumberland River and is a haven for migrating and resident songbirds and waterfowl. The photograph shows one of the park's seven rustic bridges on its five miles of paved walkways. Another five miles of primitive trails also wind through the park.*

◄ **Vinney Links:** *The golf course in Shelby Park is named for country singer Vince Gill, an avid golfer and a supporter of youth golf programs. He was instrumental in developing this nine-hole, par-twenty-nine course. Vinney Links is part of "The First Tee," a nationwide program designed to introduce young people of all backgrounds to golf.*

◀ **Opryland Hotel, Cascades:** *One of three climate-controlled, glass atriums in the Opryland Hotel, the Cascades has two restaurants, a waterfall, and dancing fountains. The three atriums hold a combined nine acres of lush gardens under glass.*

▶ **Opryland Hotel, Delta:** *The shops and restaurants in the Delta are reminiscent of the French Quarter of New Orleans. An indoor river with flatboats winds through the arcade, taking guests through the bayou-like setting.*

▶ **Opryland Hotel, Conservatory:** *The Conservatory, seen here decorated for Christmas, is surrounded by rooms with balconies overlooking tropical gardens, waterfalls, and restaurants.*

▲ **Grand Ole Opry House:** *This imposing building has been the home of the Grand Ole Opry since 1974. During the Christmas holidays, the Grand Ole Opry House is the stage for specials and the Opry moves Downtown to its original home. During the regular season, the Grand Ole Opry has three performances: Tuesday, Friday, and Saturday night shows.*

▶ **Grand Ole Opry House:** *on the stage of Grand Ole Opry, "Riders in the Sky" sing songs of the Old West in the tradition of singing cowboys such as Gene Autry, Roy Rogers, and Sons of The Pioneers. The list of performers who have graced the radio show's stage is a veritable history of American music. The Opry, first broadcasted in 1925, is the longest running live radio program in the U.S.*

GRAND OLE OPRY

WWW.OPRY.COM

▲ **Acuff Theater:** *The theater was named for the late Roy Acuff, one of the original members of Grand Ole Opry. Along with his band, The Smoky Mountain Boys, he was a foundation of both the Opry and country music as we know it today. Now part of the Opry Plaza, the theater is a modern performance hall.*

▶ **Grand Ole Opry Museum:** *Just across the plaza from the Grand Old Opry House, the museum contains exhibits from the show's long history as well as country music artifacts and a gift shop. Visitors can enjoy amazing interactive experiences that allow them to relive the history of country music while listening to the music.*

▶ **The Gibson Showcase:** *Located in Opry Mills, the showcase is a factory, a store, and a performance hall. Visitors to this 35,000-square-foot attraction can watch skilled craftsmen and women hand make Gibson mandolins and acoustic guitars. There is also a retail shop inside where Gibson instruments are sold. The entrance at the right of this photograph represents the headstock of a Gibson mandolin.*

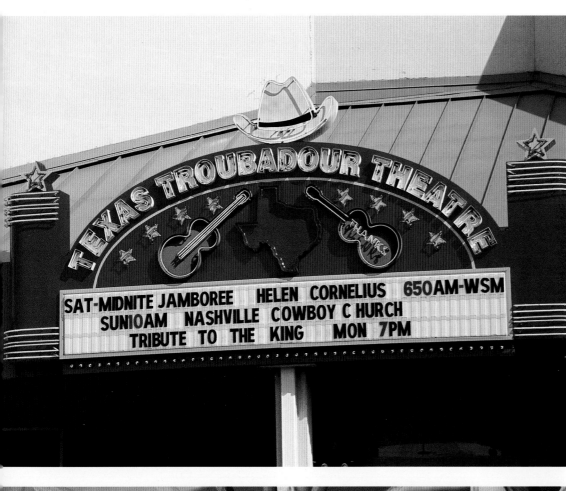

Texas Troubadour Theatre: *Next door to the Ernest Tubb Record Shop is the venue for the Midnight Jamboree. Broadcast every Saturday night, this great radio show—the second-longest running in American history—is a tradition that began Downtown in 1947 at the original Ernest Tubb Record Shop on Broadway. The theater also hosts "A Tribute to the King," a show that traces every stage of Elvis Presley's career.*

The Cowboy Church: *As well as shows, the Texas Troubadour Theatre is also used for church services. Worshippers gather at 10:00am every Sunday for non-denominational services with a Western flavor.*

▲ **The Ernest Tubb Record Shop, Number Two:** *The younger sister of Broadway's historic store is in Music Valley, near the Gaylord Opryland complex. Inside, the last touring bus used by Ernest Tubb and the Texas Troubadours is on permanent display. The shop has an extensive inventory of contemporary and hard-to-find recordings as well as sheet music and books.*

◄ **Two Rivers Mansion:** *Situated east of Music Valley on McGavock Pike, between the Cumberland and the Stones rivers, this was the last antebellum plantation house to be built in Nashville. Construction began on the eve of the Civil War and was not completed until the 1870s. Nearly 250 years later, it is operated by the Metro Parks Department for tours and special events. Its romantic setting and old world charm make Two Rivers a favorite location for Nashville weddings.*

▶ **The Hermitage:** *Andrew Jackson built his home, the Hermitage, eleven miles east of Nashville on 225 acres of land he purchased in 1804 from original settler Nathaniel Hays. The price was $3,400. As well as cotton, Jackson's cash crop, the farm also grew food for the family and slaves, and Jackson also indulged his passion for breeding racehorses here. The farm's house is now the third most-visited presidential museum in the country. Well-informed docents in period dress conduct daily tours of the mansion and grounds.*

◀ **Hermitage:** *Andrew and Rachel Jackson lived out their lives at the Hermitage, which Jackson originally called his "rural retreat." The first house, which had been built by Hays, was a simple log cabin. After Jackson became president, Nashville architect David Morris designed a more fitting house. In 1834 fire nearly destroyed the mansion, but it was rebuilt in its present style.*

◀ **Alfred's Cabin:** *Alfred Jackson was born a slave at the Hermitage. His cabin is located behind the main house and is the only remaining slave house on the grounds, though by 1820 the farm was worked by ninety-five slaves. After emancipation Alfred stayed on as a tenant farmer and became the first tour guide when the Hermitage was opened to the public. The man who lived at the Hermitage longer than anyone, white or black, died in 1901 and was buried in the Jackson cemetery.*

▲ **Hermitage Church:**
Andrew Jackson and a few of his neighbors donated money to build this simple country church in 1854. The original nine-member congregation named it Ephesus Church. It is located on the grounds of Tulip Grove, part of the Hermitage property.

West Nashville

The west side of Nashville, from Sixteenth Avenue to the Williamson County line, includes the communities of West End, Belle Meade, West Meade, Sylvan Park, Bellevue, and Pasquo. It is a treasure trove of historical buildings and beautiful parklands.

The Vanderbilt University campus begins at the intersection of West End and Twenty-First Avenue. Vanderbilt was established in 1888 as a Methodist college with an endowment from industrialist Cornelius Vanderbilt. It is now a private university with an enrolment of over 11,000 full- and part-time time students. Its 350-acre campus is also a national arboretum, while just west of the campus is another of the city's finest parks—Centennial Park. Opened as a city park after the close of the state's 1897 centennial celebration, the centerpiece of Centennial Park is the breathtaking full-size replica of the Parthenon in Athens.

The community of Belle Meade, about five miles from Downtown, is situated on land that was once part of the 1,200-acre Belle Meade Plantation. This is a neighborhood of stately homes and large estates, as exemplified by Cheekwood. This beautiful house built at the end of Belle Meade Boulevard by Leslie Cheek in 1931 was paid for with Cheek's part of the forty million dollar sale of Maxwell House Coffee to the Postum Company, now General Foods. Fortunately for the public, it is now open to visitors as Cheekwood Botanical Gardens and Fine Arts Center. The main entrance to Warner Park, the city's largest, is also at the end of Belle Meade Boulevard. Warner Park is in fact two adjacent parks; Percy Warner and Edwin Warner parks. Together they form 2,684 acres of forested hills and grassy fields that include the Iroquois Steeplechase Course.

The entrance to Belle Meade Mansion, built by General William G. Harding in 1853, is just west of Belle Meade Boulevard on Harding Pike, a continuation of West End Avenue. This superb old Greek Revival house was spared serious damage during the Civil War and today stands virtually unchanged since the time it was constructed. Belle Meade, known locally as the "Queen of Plantations," became a successful thoroughbred horse farm after the Civil War. Indeed, the first American horse to win the English Derby—Iroquois—was bred here. Another champion thoroughbred, Inquirer, is buried on the grounds, and a handsome monument marks the grave. The mansion, stables, and several outbuildings are open for tours and special events.

Just west of the Harpeth River, near the Williamson County line, lies the community of Pasquo, which has the distinction of being the terminus of the Natchez Trace Parkway. The Loveless Motel opened on U.S. Highway 100 in 1951, in the days before the interstate was built and the highway was the main route from Nashville to Memphis. Its days as a working motel have passed, but something of its old atmosphere remains, and today the Loveless Motel and Café is a country-style restaurant specializing in Southern food.

▶ **Vanderbilt University:** *Kirkland Hall on West End Avenue houses the office of the Chancellor and other administrative services. It dates back to 1875, but the first building was nearly destroyed by fire in 1905. When it was rebuilt, the architects decided to discard its original Victorian Gothic style in favor of an Italianate look. The clock tower is based on that of the Town Hall in Siena, Italy.*

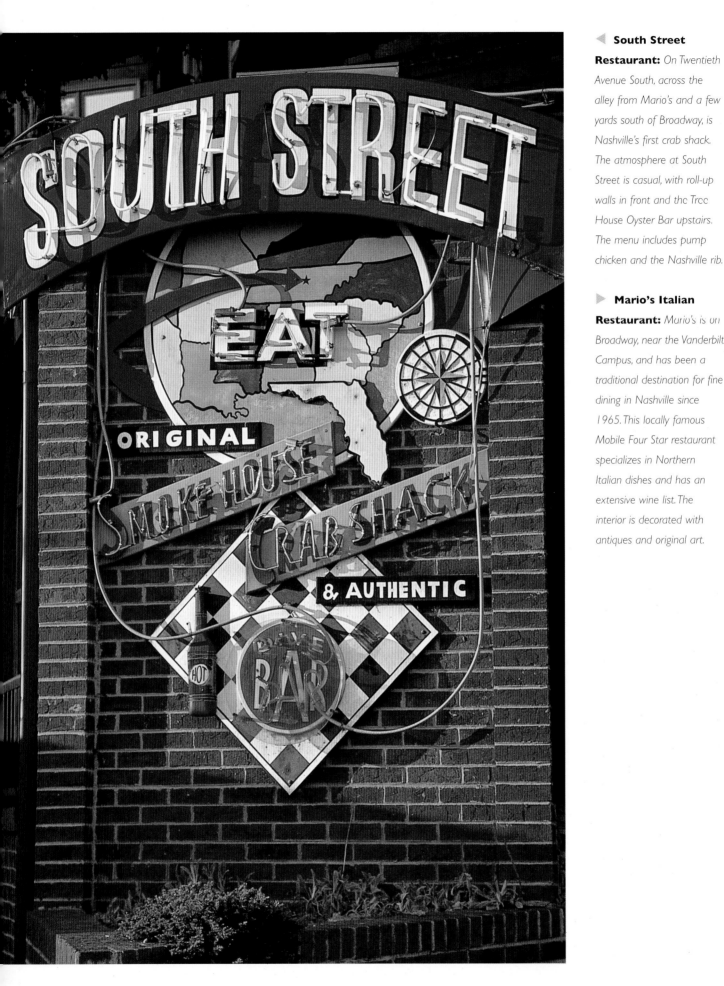

◄ South Street Restaurant: *On Twentieth Avenue South, across the alley from Mario's and a few yards south of Broadway, is Nashville's first crab shack. The atmosphere at South Street is casual, with roll-up walls in front and the Tree House Oyster Bar upstairs. The menu includes pump chicken and the Nashville rib.*

► Mario's Italian Restaurant: *Mario's is on Broadway, near the Vanderbilt Campus, and has been a traditional destination for fine dining in Nashville since 1965. This locally famous Mobile Four Star restaurant specializes in Northern Italian dishes and has an extensive wine list. The interior is decorated with antiques and original art.*

◀ **Jimmy Kelley's:**
*Nashville's premier
steakhouse since 1934 is
Jimmy Kelley's on Louise
Avenue, one block north of
Elliston Place. The current
owner, Mike Kelley, continues
his family's tradition of
Southern hospitality, steaks,
and seafood, and still serves
the restaurant's specialty—
hot mini corncakes.*

▲ **Elliston Place Soda
Shop:** *A fixture in this West
End neighborhood since
1939, Elliston Place remains
practically unchanged. In
addition to being an ice
cream and sandwich shop, it
is locally known as a "meat
and three." The term comes
from its plate lunches, which
consist of meat selection and
three vegetables. Southern
lunches are typically
accompanied by a tall glass
of iced tea.*

▶ **Fannie Mae Dees
Park:** *Better known as
Dragon Park to neighborhood
children who play on the
giant sea serpent, Fanny Mae
Dees Park is at the corner of
Blakemore and Twenty-Fourth
Avenue South, adjacent to
the Vanderbilt University
Medical Center campus. The
serpent was created by artist
Pedro Silva who made the
surface beneath from cork to
ensure the safety of the
children.*

▲ **Centennial Park, Parthenon:** *To insure the accuracy of the reliefs on the east and west pediments, casts were made of the Elgin Marbles, the remnants of the original Parthenon, which are housed in the British Museum, London. The copies of the Elgin Marbles are now on permanent exhibit together with a forty-two-foot reproduction of Athena. Centennial Park on West End Avenue, about two miles west of Downtown, was originally the site of the 1897 Tennessee Centennial Exposition. After the exposition closed, the grounds were turned into a city park.*

▶ **Centennial Park:**
A memorial to John W. Thomas, president of the Nashville, Chattanooga and St. Louis railroad, and also president of the Centennial Exposition, stands on the southwest lawn of the Parthenon. Railroad employees commissioned the statue in 1907.

◀ **Centennial Park, Arts Festival:** *The park hosts art and cultural festivals throughout the year. Works by local and regional potters, wood carvers, weavers, and traditional folk artists are a common sight. Musical performances on the grounds and concerts in the band shell give strollers a taste of jazz, blues, urban, classical, folk and, of course, country.*

▶ **Centennial Park, Civil War Monument:** *This memorial in the park to "The Heroism of the Private Confederate Soldier" was commissioned by the Association of Confederate Veterans in 1909. The engraved motto reads "Duty Done, Honor Won."*

◀ **Centennial Park, Australian Festival:** *This game of Australian football on the south lawn of the Parthenon is part of the Australian Festival. The vast green is also the best place in the city to fly kites and toss frisbees, as well as being a popular retreat for Vanderbilt University students.*

ERECTED 1909
BY

FRANK CHEATHAM BIVOUAC NUMBER 1
ASSOCIATION OF CONFEDERATE SOLDIERS
CAMP NUMBER 35
UNITED CONFEDERATE VETERANS
NASHVILLE, TENNESSEE

◀▲ **Cheekwood**

Mansion: *Leslie Cheek built Cheekwood as a private home in 1931. He was a principal in Cheek and Neal Coffee Company, which produced a blended coffee named for Nashville's Maxwell House Hotel. Maxwell House Coffee was sold in 1928 for forty million dollars and Leslie Cheek used his share of the proceeds to build this magnificent estate. It was offered to the city as a site for a botanical and art museum by Cheek's family in the 1950s, and today is a center of European and American art with over 600 paintings in the permanent collection, as well as a large sculpture collection. Spread over fifty-five acres, the grounds contain beautiful ornamental gardens, including the original boxwood garden.*

◄ **Cheekwood,
Botanical Gardens:**

*Cheekwood was deeded to
the Tennessee Botanical
Gardens and Fine Art Center
in 1959 by the Cheek family.
Today the grounds are
landscaped as part of the
vast botanical gardens. This
reflecting pool is in the center
of the original boxwood
garden.*

▲ **Cheekwood,
Botanical Gardens:**
*Botanical Hall is the
centerpiece of eight gardens,
each with a special theme.
This is the Japanese Garden,
at the end of a meandering
path that passes through a
bamboo grove. Botanical Hall
is the hub of horticultural
events and the annual winter
Festival of the Holidays.*

▶ **Cheekwood,
Botanical Gardens:** *The
"Guardian" is one of many
sculptures placed about the
fifty-five-acre grounds of
Cheekwood. The stone owl
was a gift from a Cheekwood
patron.*

◀ **Belle Mead Mansion:** *Meaning "beautiful meadow," Belle Meade is the name General William G. Harding gave his 1,200-acre plantation on Harding Pike, seven miles from Downtown Nashville. The house was completed in 1853 and survived the Civil War intact. Built in the Greek Revival style that was popular at the time, the mansion is furnished with period pieces, many of which are original to the residence. The mansion, stables, and grounds are open daily for tours and special events.*

▲ **Woodlawn:** *Woodlawn was built in 1823 for Captain John Nichols, about three miles west of Downtown on what is now West End Avenue. Andrew Jackson and Sam Houston were both friends of Captain Nichols and were frequent guests here. The house was remodeled in 1900 to face Woodmont Boulevard, and today it houses the law firm of attorney Randal L. Kinnard.*

◀ **Belle Meade, Slave Cabins:** *These huts are replicas of the housing provided for slaves on the Belle Meade plantation. The original slave quarters have long since vanished, but parts of similar dwellings were moved here to construct these cabins as museum, and interpretive centers. After the Civil War, some freed slaves remained at Belle Meade as employees.*

▶ **Belle Meade, Grave of Enquirer:** *Belle Meade became recognized as a thoroughbred horse farm in the last twenty-five years of the nineteenth century. Three of the estate's most renowned sires were Iroquois, Enquirer, and Bonnie Scotland. Even today most Kentucky Derby winners can trace their bloodlines to Bonnie Scotland. This monument marks the grave of Enquirer.*

◀ **Belle Meade, Log Cabin:** *This cabin dates from the time when Belle Meade was known as Dunham Station. General Harding's parents, John and Suzan Harding, purchased 250 acres on the Old Natchez Road in 1807 and built this "dog-trot" log cabin as their home. The name is derived from the open center part of the cabin separating the kitchen from the main room. Small sleeping rooms were in the loft.*

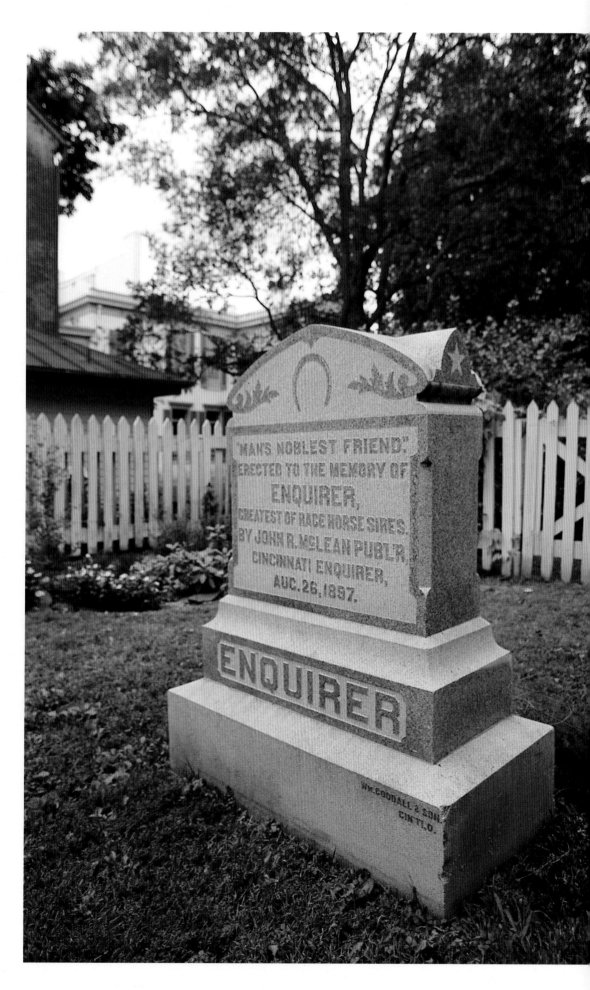

▶ **Percy Warner Park, Steeplechase Course:** *Built in 1936 by the Works Progress Administration, the Iroquois Steeplechase has been held on this course in Percy Warner Park on the second Saturday in May since 1941. The races are held over a three-mile course of wood, water, and brush jumps.*

◀ **Edwin Warner Park, Nature Center:** *On U.S. Highway 100 at Edwin Warner Park is this environmental education facility and interpretive center. It is also the starting point for hiking trails throughout the combined 2,684 acres of Percy Warner and Edwin Warner parks.*

▶ **Percy Warner Park, Steeple Chase Grounds:** *The Iroquois Bell in front of the stables is only rung on race day, and is painted in the colors of the winner until the following year. Since 1981, the Iroquois Steeplechase has been a major fundraiser for Vanderbilt Children's Hospital, raising hundreds of thousands of dollars annually.*

▲▲ **Percy Warner Park, Iroquois Steeple Chase:** *A favorite event for the audience of over 50,000 spectators at the annual steeplechase is the parade of the Hillsboro Hounds. It signals the last race of the day, the Iroquois itself.*

▲ **Percy Warner Park, Harpeth Hills Golf Course:** *Next to the steeplechase grounds on Old Hickory Boulevard in Percy Warner Park, this challenging eighteen-hole, par-seventy-two course is one of seven golf courses in the Metro Nashville Parks system.*

▶ **Chaffin's Barn Dinner Theater:** *The oldest professional theater in Nashville is located on U.S. Highway 100, just west of the Harpeth Scenic River. Since 1967, Chaffin's has offered Southern-style buffet dinners and theater in the round in a quiet country setting.*

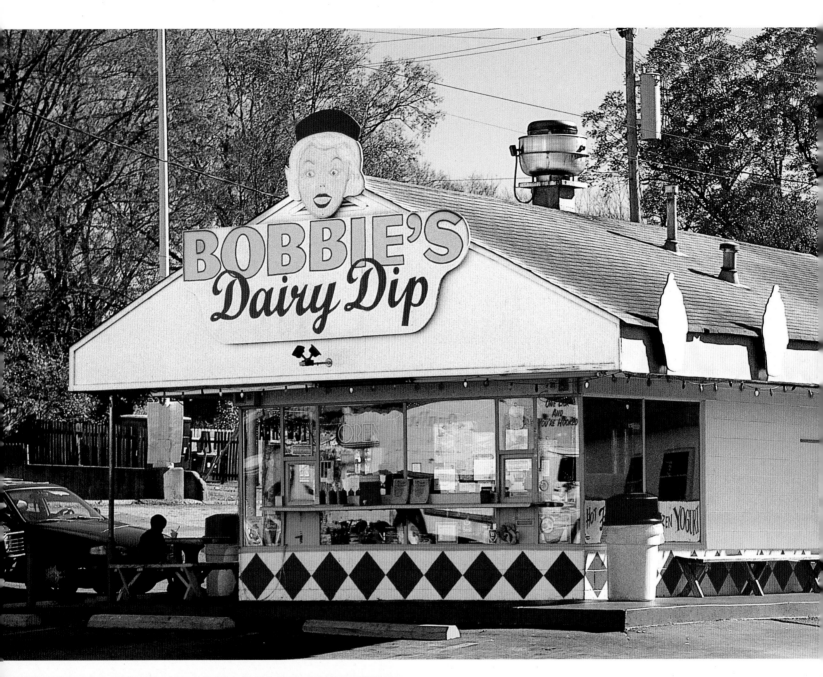

◀ **Loveless Motel:** *Lon and Annie Loveless opened their motel in 1951 on U.S. Highway 100. Before they built a proper restaurant, Lon put picnic tables in the front yard and sold Annie's fried chicken to travelers. Though it now has new owners, the Loveless Motel and Café is still known for the its fried chicken and for the country biscuits made with Annie's secret recipe.*

▲ **Bobbie's Dairy Dip:** *You can still get burgers, fries, and milk shakes at this old-fashioned neighborhood drive-in, and as a new twist on fries, Bobbie's offers them made from sweet potatoes and served with a sweet-sour cream sauce. Bobbie's is located on Charlotte Pike in West Nashville, one of the city's "rediscovered" neighborhoods.*

▶ **Loveless Café:** In Middle Tennessee, people take their food seriously. The traditional barbeque is made by slow cooking pork shoulder over hickory coals. But while Memphis-style barbeque is slathered with sauce, here it is served on the side. At the Loveless Café it is cooked outdoors in the fresh air under this screened Bar-B-Q house.

Index

Map of Nashville

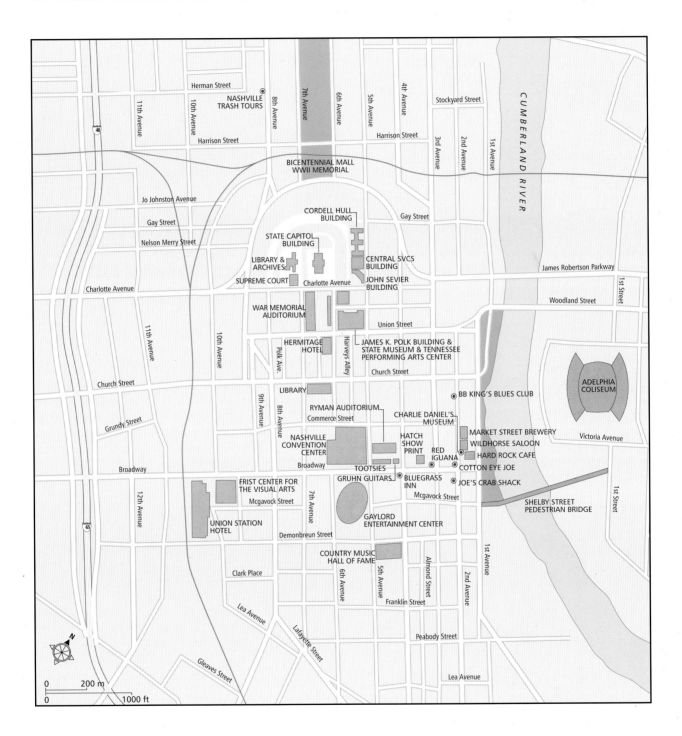

Herman Street

11th Avenue
10th Avenue
8th Avenue
7th Avenue
6th Avenue
5th Avenue
4th Avenue
3rd Avenue
2nd Avenue
1st Avenue

NASHVILLE TRASH TOURS

Stockyard Street

Harrison Street
Harrison Street

CUMBERLAND RIVER

BICENTENNIAL MALL
WWII MEMORIAL

Jo Johnston Avenue

Gay Street

CORDELL HULL
BUILDING

Gay Street

James Robertson Parkway

Nelson Merry Street

STATE CAPITOL
BUILDING

1st Street

Charlotte Avenue

LIBRARY &
ARCHIVES

CENTRAL SVCS
BUILDING

Woodland Street

SUPREME COURT

Charlotte Avenue

JOHN SEVIER
BUILDING

11th Avenue

10th Avenue

WAR MEMORIAL
AUDITORIUM

Union Street

Church Street

HERMITAGE
HOTEL

Polk Ave.

Harveys Alley

JAMES K. POLK BUILDING &
STATE MUSEUM & TENNESSEE
PERFORMING ARTS CENTER

Church Street

ADELPHIA
COLISEUM

LIBRARY

BB KING'S BLUES CLUB

Grundy Street

9th Avenue

8th Avenue

RYMAN AUDITORIUM

CHARLIE DANIEL'S
MUSEUM

Commerce Street

Victoria Avenue

MARKET STREET BREWERY

WILDHORSE SALOON

Broadway

NASHVILLE
CONVENTION
CENTER

HATCH
SHOW
PRINT

RED
IGUANA

HARD ROCK CAFE

COTTON EYE JOE

12th Avenue

Broadway

TOOTSIES

GRUHN GUITARS

BLUEGRASS
INN

JOE'S CRAB SHACK

FRIST CENTER
FOR
THE VISUAL ARTS

Mcgavock Street

7th Avenue

Mcgavock Street

1st Street

SHELBY STREET
PEDESTRIAN BRIDGE

UNION STATION
HOTEL

GAYLORD
ENTERTAINMENT CENTER

Demonbreun Street

Clark Place

COUNTRY MUSIC
HALL OF FAME

6th Avenue

5th Avenue

Almond Street

Franklin Street

2nd Avenue

1st Avenue

Lea Avenue

Lafayette Street

Peabody Street

Gleaves Street

Lea Avenue

N

0   200 m
0   1000 ft